A School Year of
POEMS

180 Favorites from Highlights

Selected and annotated with teaching ideas by
Walter B. Barbe, PhD

Illustrated by Dennis Hockerman

Boyds Mills Press

In memory of
Paul A. Witty,
friend of children and lover of poetry
—W. B. B.

Compilation and original text copyright © 2005 by Walter B. Barbe, PhD
Illustrations copyright © 2005 by Boyds Mills Press

Published by Boyds Mills Press, Inc.
A Highlights Company
815 Church Street
Honesdale, Pennsylvania 18431
Printed in China

Publisher's Cataloging-in-Publication Data

A school year of poems : 180 favorites from Highlights / selected and annotated
with teaching ideas by Walter B. Barbe ; illustrated by Dennis Hockerman.
[112] p. : ill. ; cm.
Summary: Simple poems for young readers, accompanied by teaching ideas to
improve reading skills.
ISBN 1-59078-313-1 • ISBN 1-59078-395-6 (pbk.)
1. Children's poetry, American. (1. American poetry — Collections.) I. Barbe,
Walter B. II. Hockerman, Dennis, ill. III. Highlights for Children. IV. Title.
811.54 22 PS586.3.S34 2005

First edition, 2005
The text of this book is set in 12-point New Century Schoolbook.

Visit our Web site at www.boydsmillspress.com

HC 10 9 8 7 6 5 4 3 2 1
PB 10 9 8 7 6 5 4 3 2 1

Contents

Gardens and Flowers

Weather

Humor

Holidays

Family and Friends

Wishes and Dreams

Introduction

Early in my teaching career, my students eagerly prepared for each monthly visit of Miss Johnson, a county supervisor, who made sure they could all recite the poem she had assigned for memorization the month before. As rigid as this requirement seems today, the students accepted the importance of poetry and looked forward to showing off their recitation skills. As an added bonus, the selections the children memorized undoubtedly stayed with them for life. I can still recite "This Is the House That Jack Built" from my own school days, and I suspect that the others who were in my class can, too.

When I was growing up, children were taught to read mostly by memorization, going through the same story or poem again and again until they knew every word. Over time, the sight-word method of learning to read lost favor to more analytical approaches. Today we know much more about children's learning styles and how they learn to read. Nevertheless, memorization still has its place—for learning the multiplication tables, how to spell certain words, and favorite poems.

For me, each poem that I have learned is like a familiar friend. I associate it with certain events and experiences in my life, and I relive those times by recalling the poem. I am fortunate to have been introduced early in life to the rhythm and rhyme of poetry, which has been a continuing source of pleasure.

There is no better way to begin the school day than by reading a poem aloud. Whether recited by an adult or by a child, poetry offers children a unique way to explore and enjoy language. Talking about the subject of and the meaning of words in a poem, repeating favorite lines of a poem, or memorizing a poem allows a child to claim language as his or her own. The lilting quality of poetry makes it easy to remember, and the satisfaction of learning a poem by heart can be rewarding in itself.

This collection of 180 easy-to-read poems from *Highlights for Children* magazine is designed for elementary-school teachers and their students to encourage listening, to increase vocabulary, and to expand both listening and reading comprehension. The poems are grouped by themes that are of interest to young children throughout the year. The accompanying skills notes offer simple exercises that relate the enjoyment of poetry to learning to read.

Introducing a Poem: The Four R's

Poetry is foremost an auditory experience, so it is particularly well suited to beginning readers. Here is the sequence of steps to introducing a poem to young children.

1. **Read Aloud** Until a word is in a child's listening vocabulary, it cannot become part of his or her reading vocabulary. To begin to recognize and enjoy poetry, children need to hear it spoken. Read the poem aloud so that they can hear the rhythm, the correct phrasing, and the pronunciation of unfamiliar words. (Before reading the poem aloud, preview with the children any possible new words either by reciting them, pointing them out on the page, or writing them on the chalkboard.)

2. **Read Along** Once the class has heard the poem read aloud a few times, the children can try reading along in unison, imitating what they have heard. This technique, called choral reading, allows all levels of readers to participate without embarrassment.

3. **Read Alone** After several rounds of listening to the poem read aloud and then reading aloud in unison, the children can try to read the poem aloud by themselves. Be sure to repeat the first two steps enough times so that children can be successful. If a child has difficulty with any word, supply the word immediately to avoid interrupting the flow of language.

4. **Recite** There are various approaches to memorizing a poem. Three of the best:

- Read the entire poem over and over (looking away from the page as phrases and sentences are remembered) until the entire poem can be recited.

- Read and learn one line at a time, adding another line and repeating it with the lines already learned.

- Use meaning to remember a poem. If the poem is about the four seasons, first learn the sequence in which the seasons are presented. If it has action, first learn the sequence of the action.

While the poetry in this collection can be an excellent tool for teaching and reinforcing specific reading skills, it is, above all, meant to be enjoyed. In that spirit, I hope that these poems—from animal antics to children's wishes and dreams—will touch children with the lasting beauty of our language.

—*Walter B. Barbe, PhD*

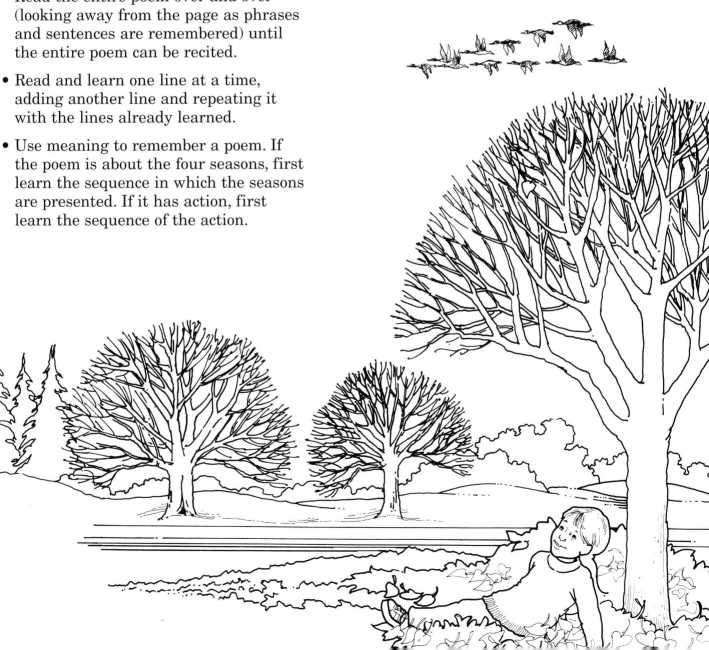

Suggestions for Teachers

Below is a list of themes and skill-building exercises that can be used with the poems in this book, along with the page number for each. Some exercises reinforce reading skills. Others suggest more general ways to help children understand and increase their enjoyment of poetry.

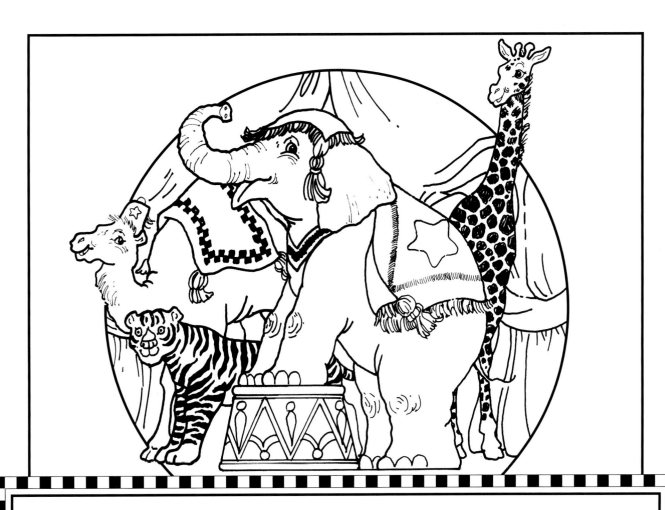

Animals

The Elephants

Swaying, swaying,
Trunks and tails,
Hay for fodder,
Water pails;
Peanuts, popcorn,
Trumpets blow,
Wiggle waggle,
Sawdust show.

— *Jacob Kisner*

I Envy the Chimp

Oh, I envy the chimp,
For he makes quite a stir
As he ambles about
In his custom-made fur.

Oh, I envy the chimp
For his devil-may-care,
Unhurried, unworried,
Unflappable air.

Oh, I envy the chimp,
For he keeps himself trim
And never gets worried
When out on a limb.

Oh, I envy the chimp;
Not a trick does he lack.
His arms are so long
He can scratch his own back.

—*Jacob Kisner*

Ridiculous Animals

Way down south where bananas grow,
A grasshopper stepped on an elephant's toe.
The elephant said, with tears in his eyes,
"Pick on somebody your own size."

—*Anonymous*

10

To a Giraffe

If I had a long,
Steep neck like you,
I know exactly
What I'd do—
I'd stand and hold
Myself quite still
So children could slide
Down my long, long hill!

—*Violet Thomas Hartmann*

Kangaroo Mother

The kangaroo mother has a pocket
  In her soft, warm skin
For her little baby
  To rest and snuggle in.

—*Maud B. Spangenburg*

For beginning readers, the effort of recognizing and pronouncing individual words correctly often interferes with comprehension. Reading aloud to children a very short poem such as "Kangaroo Mother" or "Ridiculous Animals," which contain familiar words, imagery, and themes, allows them to grasp the sound and meaning of the poem before trying to read along or read the poem themselves.

Frogs

Beside my pool with lilies in it,
  The spotted frogs amuse me.
Although they do a burp a minute,
  They never say "Excuse me."

—Strickland Gillilan

The Itchy Back

What do you suppose the turtle does
In a house he can't unlatch
When he has an itch
Upon his back
That he cannot reach to scratch?

—Jean Chisholm

Repetition of words and phrases is a common device in poetry. In "Dabbling Ducks" on page 13, ask the children to find the two words that are repeated (*dabble, gabble*) and to tell the beginning sound of each word. Another type of repetition is alliteration, when initial consonant sounds are repeated in two or more neighboring words or syllables. Five of the eight lines of "The Elephants" on page 9 contain alliteration.

Dabbling Ducks

Time to sup,
Tails all up.
   Gabble! Gabble! Gabble!
Things to eat,
Good and sweet.
   Dabble! Dabble! Dabble!

Like a clown,
Heads all down,
   Feet and tail a-quiver.
Sakes alive!
See them dive
   In the whirly river.

Tails all up,
Time to sup.
   Gabble! Gabble! Gabble!
There they go
Down below.
   Dabble! Dabble! Dabble!

—*Nona Keen Duffy*

The Tipped-Up Duck

The underside of an up-end duck
Is soft . . .
And white.

He dives for his lunch in the mud and muck
From morn . . .
Till night.

In a headstand he never does get stuck,
But then . . .
He might.

—*Lucile Maxfield Bogue*

My Dog

My dog is lots of company
  When I am all alone,
But he is too much company
  When I have an ice-cream cone.

—Marguerite Hamilton

Pals

He sits and begs; he gives a paw;
He is, as you can see,
The finest dog you ever saw,
And he belongs to me.

He follows everywhere I go
And even when I swim.
I laugh because he thinks, you know,
That I belong to him.

—Arthur Guiterman

14

My Friend

I have a silent company,
A friend who cannot talk.
I lay my hand upon his head
When we go for a walk.

I tell him dreams and troubles
And he seems to understand,
For he nuzzles up and gently
Lays his paw upon my hand.

His brown eyes look up trustingly
And say, plain as can be,
"Whatever you want or think or do
Is sure OK with me!"

—*Helen Rosina*

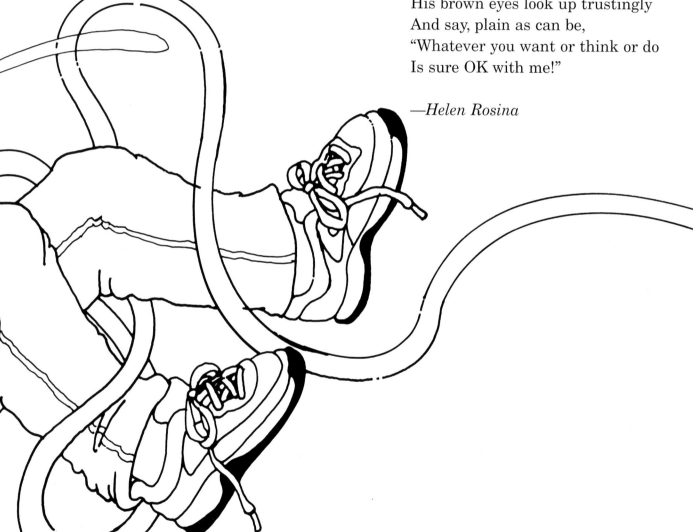

 These three short poems about dogs provide an opportunity to demonstrate to young readers who habitually skip or add words that the rhythm of the poem will help them in reading it. For example, in the poem "Pals," if the child misread the third line as "The finest dog in the whole world," the rhyme would be broken and the rhythm of the poem noticeably thrown off.

Happy Talk

A goose can honk like an automobile.
A snake can hiss
Like this-s-s-s-s-s.

An owl can hoot like a railroad train.
A bee can buzz
And does-z-z-z-z-z-z.

A cow can moo like an old foghorn.
What pigeons do
Is coo-oo-oo-oo-oo-oo.

A parrot can talk like a human,
But I am sure
The purr-r-r-r-r-r
That I hear when I stroke my kitty
Is nicer than hisses, buzzes, or coos.
It's pretty.

—*Ruth Manley Powers*

Kittens

Guess what I found in the hamper—
    Kittens so small and wee.
And to whom do you think the kittens belong?
    To the cat that belongs to me!

—*Harriet Evatt*

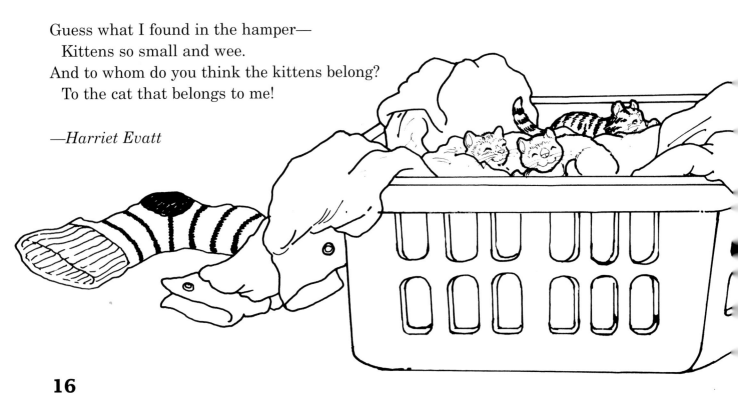

16

Moving Day

When Mother Cat decides to move,
She acts so very proud.
She finds a home and doesn't care
If cats are not allowed.

She moves her kittens, one by one,
According to her plan.
She carries them and doesn't need
To call a moving van.

—*Jacqueline Selzer*

Even though poetry is primarily an auditory tool, emphasizing rhythm, it can also help to reinforce the visual and kinesthetic skills of reading from left to right. Using "Moving Day," have the children place their finger on the first word of the poem, the second word, and so on to the last as they read aloud. Each sentence begins on one line and ends on the next line below, sweeping back and forth from left to right.

Mice's Song

Cheese-on-toast
  delights us most.
Please leave a little
  beneath the table.
Cracker-and-cheese
  are sure to please,
And we shall eat
  as much as we're able.
Cheeseless food
  is not so good,
But if we're hungry,
  we wouldn't mind it.
Whatever's to spare
  please leave it where
It's easiest for
  us mice to find it.

—Ivy O. Eastwick

18

A Mouse Tale

A mouse
Has a house
In the wall,
With a door
Near the floor—
Not tall
And very thin,
So the cat
Can't get in.

—*Sr. Saint Simon*

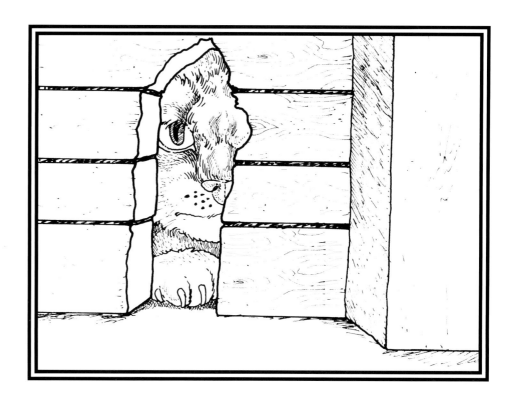

The Mouse

All dressed in gray,
A little mouse
Has made his home
Within my house.
And every night
And every morn
I say, "I wish
That mouse were gone."
But why? A quiet soul is he
As anyone might wish to see.
My house is large,
My hearth is wide,
There's room for him
And me beside.

—*Anonymous*

For beginning readers, write the poem "The Mouse" on the chalkboard or a piece of paper and ask the children to find how many lines begin with the letter *a* (in this case, six). Repeat with other letters and other poems. Depending on their maturity, the children can also look for beginning letters on words within the poem, or look for words ending with the same letter.

The Magic Cow

I marvel at the lazy cow,
For I cannot discover how
She manages so well to hide
So many bottles of milk inside.

—*Ilo Orleans*

Please!

Give me a horse
I can ride to town,
Up, down!
Up, down!
A horse I can feed
Both sugar and hay,
Then gallop and gallop
And gallop away.
No matter what color—
Gray, spotted, or roan—
But give me a horse
For my very own.

—*Clarice Foster Booth*

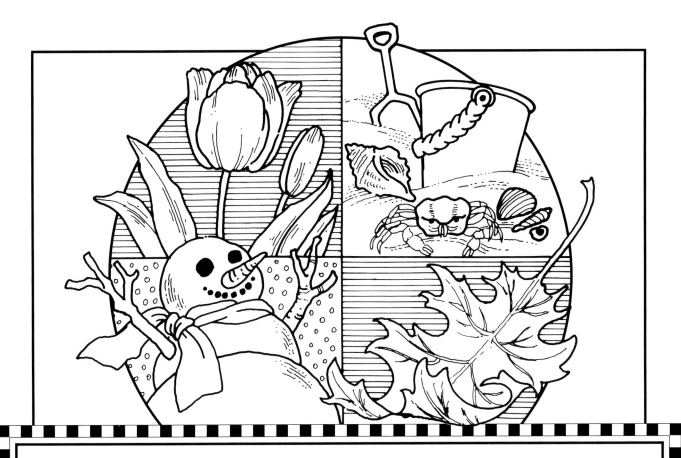

Seasons

Spinning Wheel

Summer is over—
the leaves drift down
over the country
and over the town,
red leaves and gold leaves,
yellow and brown.

Autumn is over—
the leaves are lost,
branches of tall trees
shimmer with frost,
snowflakes are falling,
a silvery host.

Winter is over—
see! A blue wing
spreads wide and rises
above everything,
songbirds and flowers
tell us it's spring.

Springtime is over—
look! Everywhere
roses and lilies
and larkspurs appear,
songbirds call gaily:
"Summer is here!"

—*Ivy O. Eastwick*

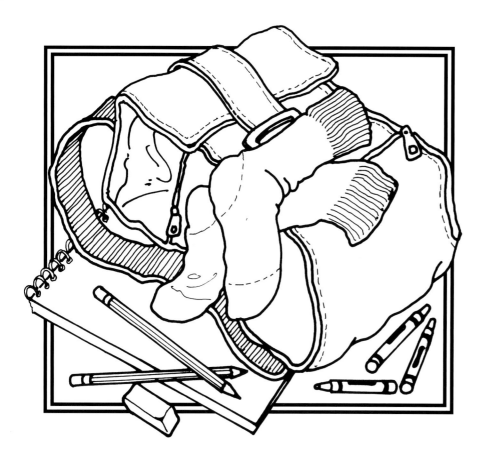

Schooltime

Days are getting shorter,
Mornings growing cool.
Mother says it's time to think
Of going back to school.

Time to buy erasers
And pencils in a box;
Time to buy new school shoes
And different-colored socks.

Time to say good-bye again
To all the summer fun.
Time to think of school because
September has begun.

—*Marian Kennedy*

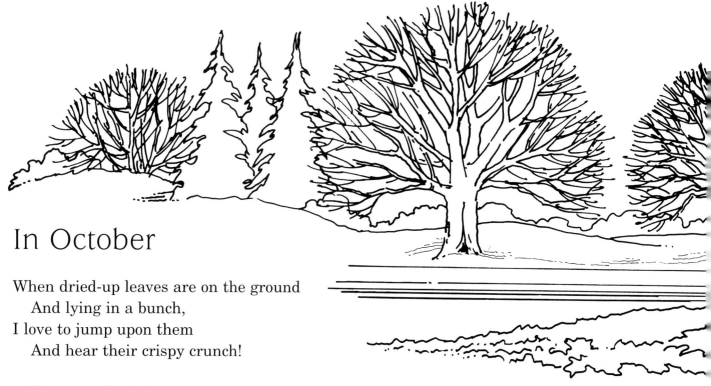

In October

When dried-up leaves are on the ground
    And lying in a bunch,
I love to jump upon them
    And hear their crispy crunch!

—*Vivian G. Gouled*

The most obvious sign to young children that a selection is a poem is the rhyming. After reading each poem on these pages aloud and having the children read along with you, ask them to pick out the rhyming words in each. The rhyming pairs use familiar, simple words (*cool / school, box / socks, go / snow*). To reinforce the meaning of rhyme, ask the children to come up with other words that rhyme with the words in the poems.

Wild Geese

Why do the wild geese leave?
  Who is it bids them go,
Warning them always of Winter,
  Whispering softly of snow?

—Harriet Evatt

Autumn Trees

There's one leaf left
  On the tip of our tree;
And across the street
  Their tree has three.

Now I wonder why
  A dozen or more
Are still left on
  The tree next door.

—Mildred Dingle Reed

Leaf Time

Oh, I loved April
When April was here!
  The quick-dropping showers,
  The little new flowers,
The fresh-sprinkled springtime,
The new-growing-thing time—
  Yes, I loved April
  When April was here!

But oh, I love scuffling
Through leaves in the fall!
  Some colored the same
  As a bonfire flame.
A crisp-crinkled brief time
Of shuff-scuffle leaf time—
  There's no finer
  Season than fall!

—*Juanita Davison*

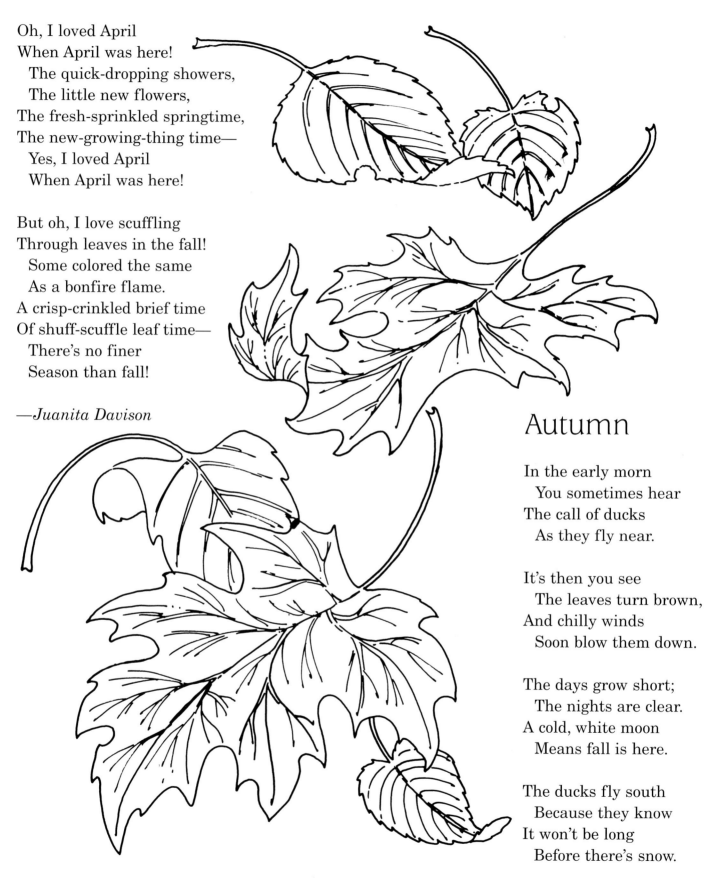

Autumn

In the early morn
  You sometimes hear
The call of ducks
  As they fly near.

It's then you see
  The leaves turn brown,
And chilly winds
  Soon blow them down.

The days grow short;
  The nights are clear.
A cold, white moon
  Means fall is here.

The ducks fly south
  Because they know
It won't be long
  Before there's snow.

—*Ruth McFadden*

The Watcher

The snow fell softly all the night,
And slowly all the world went white.
So softly did the snowflakes fall
I slept and heard them not at all.
When I awoke, the land lay still
And white above my windowsill.
The smoke hung slim and straight and high
Between the chimneys and the sky.
No footsteps fell upon the street.
The silence stood on silent feet.

Long winter nights when I lie curled
Asleep—asleep—the watching world
In snowy stillness softly slips
Her whitest finger to her lips—
Sh-sh-sh-sh-sh-sh-sh!

—*Omar Lee Reed*

Children can identify poetry using visual as well as auditory clues. Visual clues arise from the way poetry is set in type, with noticeably short sentences, varied indentation, and, often, an uppercase letter at the beginning of each line. For instance, both "Leaf Time" and "Autumn" have indented lines, with an uppercase letter at the beginning of each line. In "The Watcher," each line begins with a capital but without indentation.

The Snowman

One time we had a snowman,
And he was cold as ice;
And though his eyes were bits of coal,
We thought him oh so nice.

He wore a very fancy scarf
And quite a dressy hat.
But when the sun came out, he left—
We were surprised at that!

—Harriet Evatt

Skating Song

Let's go skating on the pond
Where it's frozen very thick.
  We'll do some whirls
  And fancy twirls,
For the ice is smooth and slick.

—Nona Keen Duffy

The rhythm of the language is probably the most distinguishing feature of a poem. Young children, however, acquire rhythm only after they can recognize words and understand the meaning of a sentence. As an auditory exercise, read aloud "Skating Song" and then have the children read along. Exaggerate the rhythm and place heavy emphasis on the final words, *pond, thick, whirls, twirls,* and *slick.*

A Winter Walk

When all the woods are sleeping
  And all the squirrels are still
And I walk among the tall, bare trees
  Up the white-clad hill,

I find such joy in battling
  The ice-cold winds that blow
And come back tired and happy,
  Stamping off the snow!

—*Elizabeth Newell*

27

Winter Wind

The wind is a lion,
I hear him roar.
He rattles the window
And slams the door.

He whirls the snow
And piles it high.
He chases the clouds
Across the sky.

The trees feel him blow,
And they bend and sway
Right down to the earth
To get out of his way.

He hurries past houses
And on down the street.
He howls with glee
If the rain turns to sleet.

And when all the people
Hurry and run,
The wild wind laughs,
For he's having fun.

—*Margaret D. Larson*

Signs of Spring

Misty green shadows, pattering rain,
   Red-breasted robins returning again,
Cows deep in meadows, up to their knees,
   Blossoming orchards, humming of bees.

—*Harriet Evatt*

Freckles

Oh, spring is here!
My freckles show!
That's a sure sign that it's so.
All winter long they hide away,
But in the spring
They come to stay.
Six freckles, plain, astride my nose,
I saw today when I first rose.

—*Lucille Sylvester*

Bare Feet

In spring, the pebbles around our yard
Are very sharp and very hard.
But if I run on them quite often,
It makes the hurty edges soften.

—*Strickland Gillilan*

Knowing about accented words and syllables can help children hear and feel the rhythm of a poem. For example, using "Winter Wind," stress the last word of each line as you read it aloud and ask the children to do the same. Then shift the accent to the beginning of each sentence (often the second word) and read the poem again. Which reading best conveys the feeling of the winter wind?

When Isabel Goes to the Seashore

When Isabel goes
to the seashore,
she tiptoes
niminy-neat,
past the sea
and the spray
that dance her way
but scarcely touch
her feet.

When Jonathan goes
to the seashore,
he walks on the edge
of the sands,
till the sea and the spray
they caper his way
and splash him on feet
and hands.

When I go down
to the seashore,
I run and jump
right in,
and the sea and the spray
they leap my way
and splash me up
to the chin.

—*Ivy O. Eastwick*

Accenting the correct syllable within a word is more difficult than accenting a whole word. Select words from these poems and ask the children to pronounce them with the accent on the correct syllable and then on the wrong syllable. In "Oceanside," the word *swimmers* is correctly accented on the first syllable. When the children pronounce it with the accent on the last syllable, it sounds wrong, even silly.

Oceanside

Clams in the sand,
Mussels on the rock,
Bass in the sea,
And boats at the dock.

Swimmers in the surf,
Hikers on the dunes,
Children on the wet sand,
Digging with spoons.

—*James Steel Smith*

Ice Cream in Summer

It's not easy
eating ice cream
in the sun—
'tisn't easy
at all but—
it's fun!
It's a sort of
a race between
me and the sun—
we don't know
who will win—
so it's fun!

—*Ivy O. Eastwick*

Summer Music

I'm always glad when summer comes,
For everything in summer hums.
Grass and leaves in green young trees,
Little brooks and homing bees,
Wind and all the air outside,
Sunny hills and meadows wide,
Children's voices, rain that drums—
Oh, everything in summer hums!

—Revah Summersgill

Kites

Let us get our kites and play,
For the wind is high today.

Far above the town they'll fly
Just like airplanes in the sky.

Loose the strings and let them go
While we hold on tight below.

Up into the sky they'll sail
While each one tugs and waves its tail.

—Nona Keen Duffy

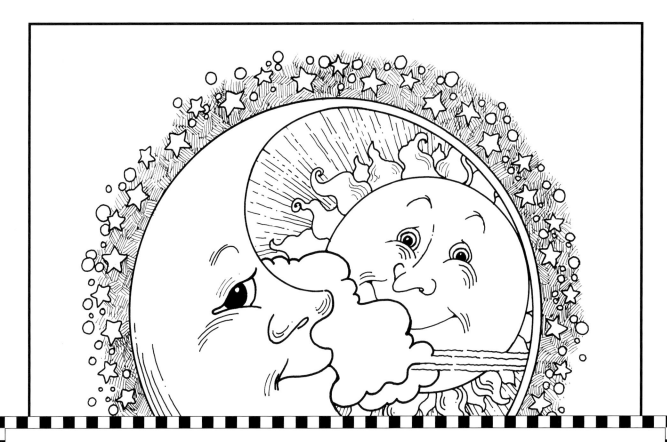

Sun, Moon, and Stars

Questions

When it's storming here on earth,
Is it lightning up on Mars?
Does it thunder on the moon?
Does it rain upon the stars?
I ask myself these questions.
They are things I'd like to know.
And some day in my spaceship
I'll learn if they are so.

—*Emily Hilsabeck*

The Wonderful Sun

Good morning, merry sunshine,
What makes you wake so soon?
You scared the little stars away
And shined away the moon.

I saw you go to sleep last night
Before I ceased my playing.
How did you get way over there,
And where have you been staying?

—Arthur M. Harding

The ability to recall the main idea of material that is read is the first goal of comprehension. A short poem, which quickly gets to the point and ends, is an ideal tool for teaching this skill. Using the poems on these pages and on page 33, ask the children to explain what each poem is about. The answer to this question in "Questions" on page 33 is clearly, What is happening in outer space?

The Sun

There's sun on the clover
  And sun on the log,
Sun on the fish pond
  And sun on the frog,

Sun on the honeybee,
  Sun on the crows,
Sun on the wash line
  To dry the clean clothes.

—*Louise Fabrice Handcock*

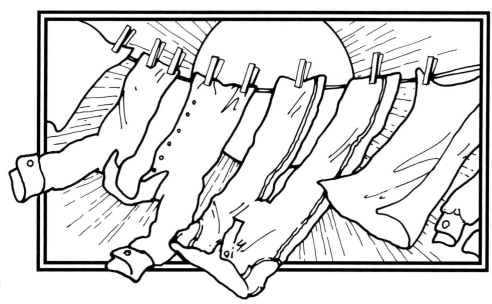

Sun and Shower

I like the sun;
I like a shower.
It takes them both
To make a flower.

Every blossom,
Blue or pink,
Very often
Needs a drink.

And each will have
A brighter hue
Because the sun
Came shining through.

—*Clarice Foster Booth*

35

Sun Magic

The sun has a wonderful bagful of tricks
And a show that runs half round the clock.
  He can lengthen the shadows
  Or shrink them to pools
Or magically waken the cock.

He can silver the lake till it loses its blue
Or glisten on windows so bright
  That every pane
  Of a skyscraper gleams
As it does when it's lighted at night.

—*Frances Zang*

At Sunset

Far down the lazy river
  The sun sinks hot and red.
Do you suppose he'd rather
  Stay up than go to bed?

Do you suppose he'd rather
  Stay up awhile and see
The big round moon, the cool white moon
  Shine through our maple tree?

I'm glad that I'm a child like me
And can see the moon through our maple tree.

—*Mary White Slater*

36

Moon Mischief

The moon was bad again last night.
I don't know what he did,
But every time I looked at him
He ran away and hid.

The sky was full of big white clouds
Like curtains everywhere,
But I could see the moon when he
Peeped through the cracks up there.

And when he saw me watching him,
He quickly hid his face,
So I am sure he must have been
In some sort of disgrace.

—*Mabel Clare Thomas*

The Moon

While playing in my yard today
I saw a little moon at play
  High overhead.

Now from my pillow I can see
That little sleepy moon, like me,
  Just going to bed!

—*Edna Becker*

Another important skill in reading comprehension is the ability to put ideas in logical sequence. Ask the children to identify the sequence of ideas in each poem on these two pages. For example, in "The Moon," the child might answer, "I was playing. I saw the moon. I went to bed. I saw the moon going to bed."

New Moon

A new moon always makes me laugh—
It wears a silly grin
Just like a jack-o'-lantern's smile
That someone cut too thin.

—*Teresa C. Sheehan*

Spilled Splendor

The moon is an empty silver dish
The clouds have tilted so high
That all the shining stars fell out
And scattered across the sky.

—*Eunice Cassidy Hendryx*

Distinguishing reality from fantasy is a comprehension skill that young children do not always automatically discover for themselves. Each of the poems on these two pages offers an opportunity to talk about this important concept. "New Moon," for example, refers to the moon's silly grin, which, in fact, is an illusion. The moon does not really laugh, as "Bedtime' declares, but the fun of the poem is in imagining that it does.

A Daytime Moon

The other day, along toward noon,
I was surprised to see the moon
   Sitting on top of a tall pine tree.

He needed the light of the sun, I guess,
For his face was pale with silverness,
   And he looked quite ill to me.

But I saw him again that very night,
And he, grown well again and bright,
   Was shining happily.

—*Wallace McElroy Kelly*

Bedtime

When I go to bed at night,
Just before I close my eyes,
I look out my window and
Watch stars blink in the skies.
Then the big, round moon looks
   down,
I think he laughs at me.
Before I close my eyes at night,
These are the things I see.

—*Edna Hamilton*

Space Trips

One time we took a trip to Mars;
Another time to Venus.
We zipped along at such a rate
We wished folks could have seen us.

Another time we went to see
The Old Man in the Moon.
But he was in a grouchy mood,
So we came back quite soon.

—Emily Hilsabeck

Reaching for Stars

Each evening when the sky is clear
 I try to pluck a star
But find that while it looks so near
 It is a bit too far.

But I will not give up. I will
 Keep trying every day.
If I don't get a star, I'll still
 Be taller, anyway.

—*Clarence Edwin Flynn*

Carnival

The night sky
Is a merry-go-round
Where the stars ride free.
The wind
Is a calliope
Playing a wild tune
On the keyboard of a tree.

—*Hildred L. Baughman*

Comprehension is the ultimate goal of reading. Using the poems on these two pages, check to see how well each child understands a poem when it is read to him or her, when the child reads it aloud, and when the child reads it silently.

Star Dippers

There are two dippers in the sky
  (At least that's what they say).
Who tipped them up and spilled the milk
  That made the Milky Way?

—*Rowena Bennett*

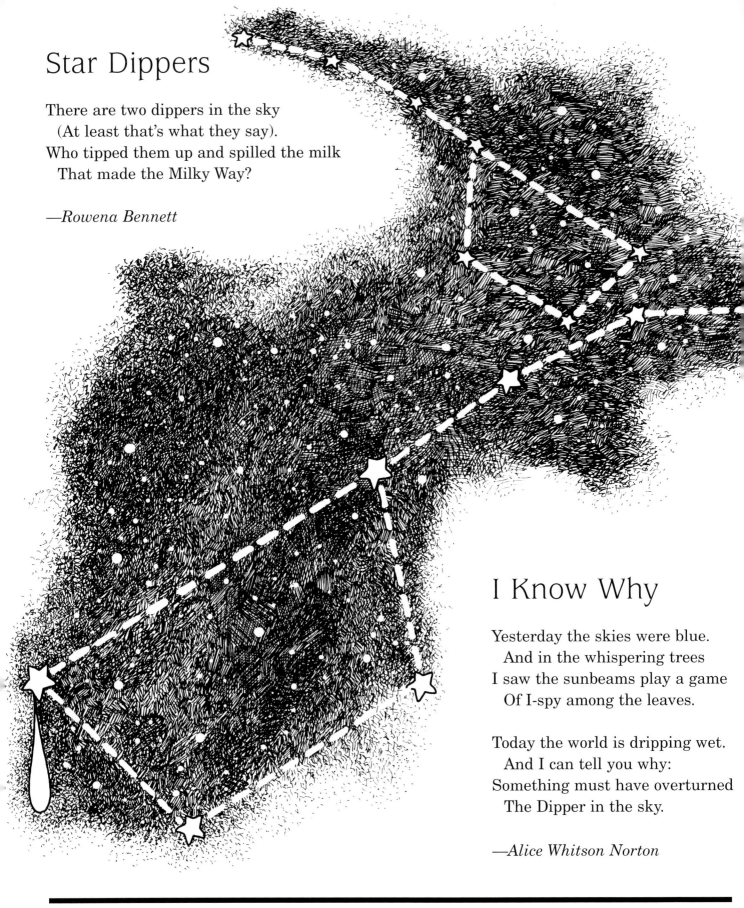

I Know Why

Yesterday the skies were blue.
  And in the whispering trees
I saw the sunbeams play a game
  Of I-spy among the leaves.

Today the world is dripping wet.
  And I can tell you why:
Something must have overturned
  The Dipper in the sky.

—*Alice Whitson Norton*

Drawing conclusions from what is read makes poetry more than merely rhythm and rhyme. After hearing and reading "Star Dippers," young children should be able to draw the conclusion that two dippers are found in the Milky Way. "Daisies" offers a good example of a fanciful conclusion: that the moon gathers the stars (daisies) and sprinkles them in the meadows.

Daisies

At evening when I go to bed
I see the stars shine overhead;
They are the little daisies white
That dot the meadow of the night.

And often while I'm dreaming so,
Across the sky the moon will go;
It is a lady, sweet and fair,
Who comes to gather daisies there.

For when at morning I arise,
There's not a star left in the skies;
She's picked them all and dropped them down
Into the meadows of the town.

—*Frank Dempster Sherman*

Star Buttons

Stars are silver buttons,
  Polished and bright,
That fasten the dark
  To the sky at night.

—*Anna P. Stone*

Homework

Tonight,
Climb up to a high roof.
Stand on the tips of your toes
As tall as you can
And let your fingers
Touch the sky.
Pick yourself a star
And pin it gently in your hair.

Go inside
And see how beautifully it shines.

Tomorrow,
Climb back to the roof
And fill your midnight hair
With stars.

—Beverly McLoughland

Gardens and Flowers

My Garden

I shall have a garden,
For today I sow my seeds,
And I will keep away the bugs
And hoe up all the weeds.

And if it doesn't rain enough,
I'll take the garden hose,
Then gently sprinkle water
All up and down the rows.

Oh, I shall have a garden
As fine as ever grew
Because I'll add a lot of love
To all the work I do.

—*Marie Small*

Winter Flowers

This is no time for gardens
  That grow beneath the sky.
But I most need a garden
  When summer has gone by.

So in a southern window,
  Safe from cold and snow,
I set a pot of hyacinths
  And watched to see them grow.

And now inside the window
  My garden is in bloom,
Bringing a breath of springtime
  Into a winter room.

—*Harriet Evatt*

The Seed

I planted just a little seed—
  No bigger than a pill.
It grew into a flower sweet
  And blooms upon my sill.

—*Grace D. Nixon*

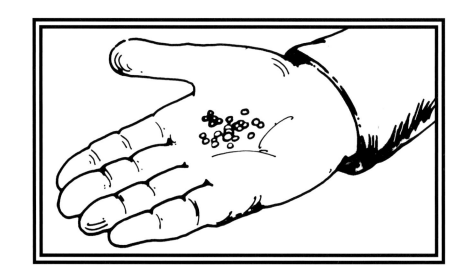

 Identifying initial consonant sounds in poetry is a good way to introduce children to phonics. List the nineteen consonant letters that make only one sound—*b, d, f, h, j, k, l, m, n, p, q, r, s, t, v, w, x, y,* and *z.* Ask the children to find each word that begins with one of these consonants in "My Garden" on page 45. Then have them write each word and read it aloud. (All of the nineteen but *j, x, y,* and *z* occur in the poems on pages 45, 46, and 47.)

Violets Know

Violets are quiet
And never make a sound
All through the winter
When they're sleeping in the ground.

But they know first when Spring comes,
And they're always there to meet her.
I wish they'd tell me how they know.
I'd be there, too, to greet her.

—*Peggy Sullivan*

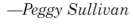

Crocus

I found a small brown onion,
  Or so it seemed to me,
But Mother said to plant it
  And see what I should see.

And so I put it in a hole
  Down in the soft, moist ground;
Then patiently I waited
  For spring to come around.

With spring, my homely onion,
  By some amazing power,
Became a yellow crocus—
  A truly lovely flower!

My mother says that people, too,
  May look so plain and old
Yet wear beneath their shabby clothes
  A heart of purest gold!

—*Harriet Evatt*

Tulip Cups

The tulip has a colored cup,
  Which every morning opens up
To catch the springtime rain and dew
  And all the golden sunshine, too.

—*Myrtle Adams*

The Rabbit

I saw it with my own two eyes
  One day just after dawn.
He came from round a lilac bush
  And hopped across the lawn.

He hopped up to the flower bed
  And nibbled at my phlox.
And then he sat up straight and nibbled
  At the hollyhocks.

And when at last he thought he had
  Enough to eat that day,
He looked at me and twitched his nose
  And
        hippity-
                hopped
                      away!

—*Ralph Marcellino*

48

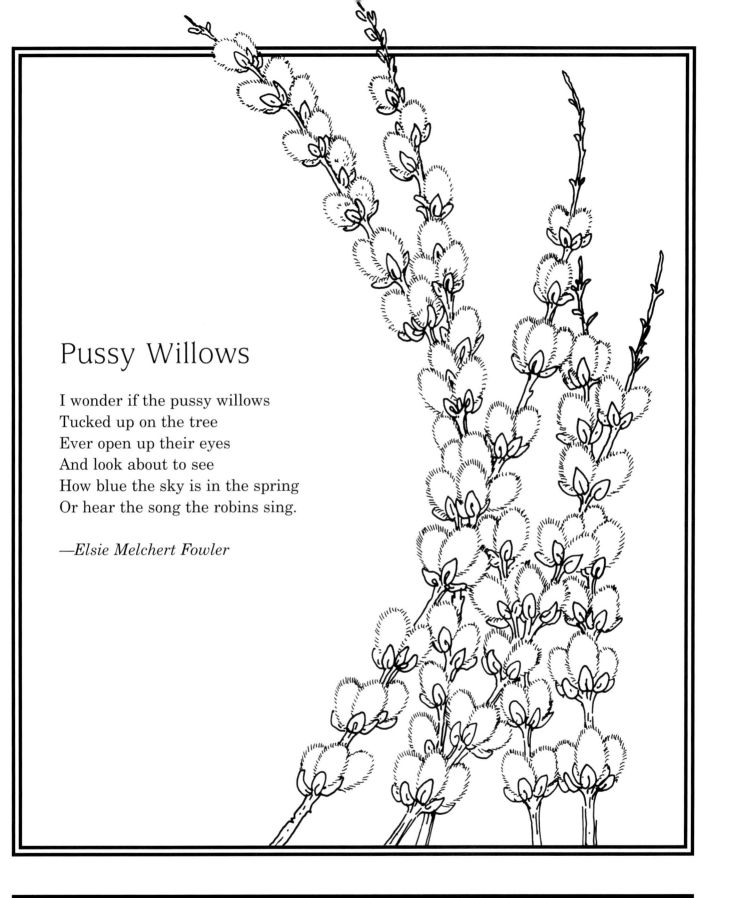

Pussy Willows

I wonder if the pussy willows
Tucked up on the tree
Ever open up their eyes
And look about to see
How blue the sky is in the spring
Or hear the song the robins sing.

—*Elsie Melchert Fowler*

The short and long vowel sounds are the most commonly used. Using the poems on these two pages, ask the children to list the words that begin with a short vowel (some are *at, ever, if, on,* and *up*) and then a long vowel (*away, enough, I,* and *opens*). Then ask the children if they can find a long-*u* word in "Valentines" on page 90 (*usual*) and "Grandma's Story-Box" on page 97 (*used*).

49

Cooked Vegetables

I planted a garden all myself—
Just rows and rows and rows
Of carrots and onions and peas and beans.
I hope each seedlet grows.

I climbed way up, awfully high,
To the topmost pantry shelf—
Up where the raisins are and such—
And took the seeds myself.

I boiled them in a saucepan good—
And, oh, how odd they looked!
Now, when my garden gets all grown,
My things will all be cooked.

—*Anna H. Hayes*

Hearing words broken into syllables helps children to understand the workings of language. As they listen when you read a poem aloud, have them tap out the syllables in each word. In "Gardening," the title has three syllables, the words *isn't*, *water*, and *garden* have two syllables, and the remaining words in the poem have only one. Repeat this for each of the other poems, checking to be certain every child is hearing the correct number of syllables.

Gardening

Isn't it fun to make seeds grow?
To plant and water, weed and hoe?
But most of all, I think, it's fun
To eat the garden when it's done.

—Ida M. Pardue

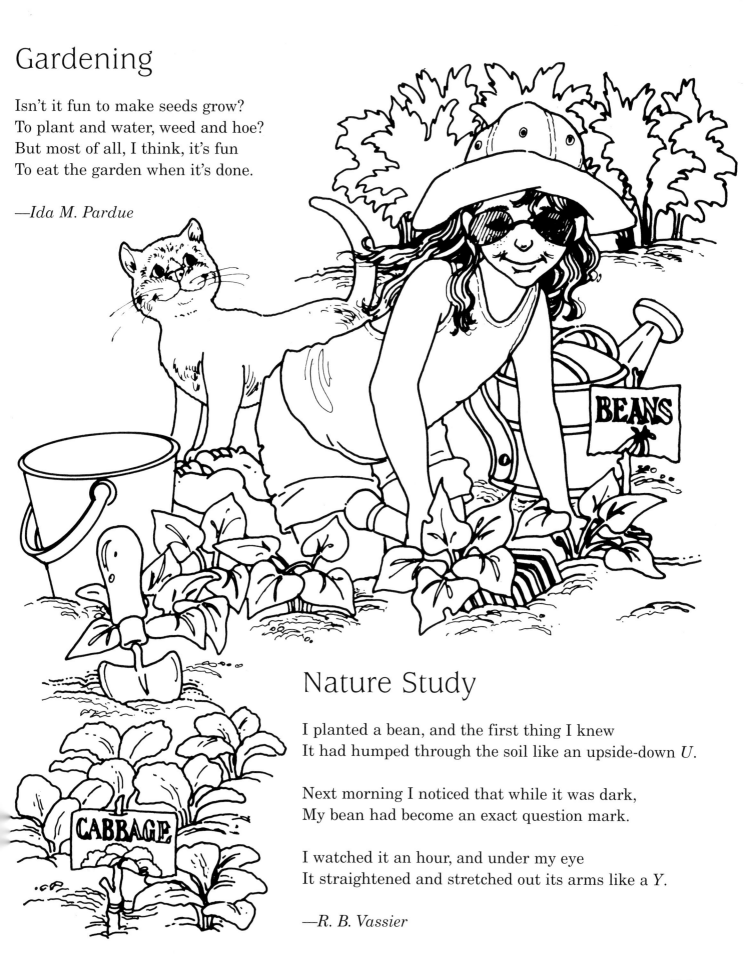

Nature Study

I planted a bean, and the first thing I knew
It had humped through the soil like an upside-down *U*.

Next morning I noticed that while it was dark,
My bean had become an exact question mark.

I watched it an hour, and under my eye
It straightened and stretched out its arms like a *Y*.

—R. B. Vassier

To a Toadstool

Folks say you are a toadstool.
But I've watched the toads to see,
And they never sit upon you;
So your name quite puzzles me!

—*Elizabeth H. Short*

Clever Nature

Eggplants are purple,
Tomatoes are red,
Lettuce is green
With a big, leafy head.

Carrots are orange,
Potatoes are brown.
(To find them you have
To dig down in the ground.)

Pumpkins are yellow.
Celery is white.
(It crunches and scrunches
With each little bite.)

Nature, I think,
Must really be smart
To give us such colorful
Vegetable art!

—*Vivian G. Gouled*

52

Following

I followed a farmer,
A plow, and a mule
Down in our garden
One day after school.
"Gee! Haw!" said the farmer.
The mule flopped its ears.
The plow cut the earth
Like a new pair of shears.

I watched robins feast
Where the soil had been turned.
I cannot tell half
Of the things that I learned
While I followed the farmer,
His plow, and his mule
Down in our garden
That day after school.

—*James S. Tippett*

The initial consonants *c* and *g* each makes two sounds. Followed by *i, e,* or *y,* the letter *c* makes the *s* sound (in "Clever Nature," the example is *celery*). Followed by *a, o,* or *u,* the letter *c* makes the *k* sound (examples on these pages are *carrots, colorful,* and *cut*). The letter *g* makes the *j* sound (*Gee* in "Following") and the hard *g* (guh) sound (*garden* in "Following"). Knowing these patterns may be of help to some children.

A Friend of Children

Shaking herself, the orchard
Scattered her petals in showers
That the children might have apples
To follow her beautiful flowers.

—Jessie May Hooker

The Apple Tree

I would like to be
As friendly as the apple tree
That spreads its branches wide
For birds to nest inside,
And starts to branch as low
As little children grow.

—Lois Leurgans

The ability to identify final sounds is an important part of phonemic awareness.
Rhyming poetry is an ideal tool for introducing this concept. After reading the poems on
these two pages aloud to the children and having them read along, point out the rhyming
patterns (for example, aa / bb / cc in "The Apple Tree") and the ending words that rhyme.
Then have the children read aloud, placing emphasis on the rhyming words.

Apple Blossoms

The blossoms on an apple tree
Are dainty, dancing dolls to me.
They fit and flutter here and there
Without a worry or a care.

—Adele Hampton

The Cherry Tree

What a lovely
  Place to be,
Underneath
  A cherry tree.

Little breezes
  Gently blow,
And soft, white petals
  Fall like snow.

The cherry blossoms
  Look like lace.
They fall like snowflakes
  On my face.

Oh, how nice
  It is to be
Underneath
  A cherry tree.

—Marian Kennedy

55

Clovers

We picked clovers for a chain
By a narrow little lane
In the pasture, for down there
We found flowers everywhere
And sticker weeds and an orange bee.
But you'd have laughed aloud to see
How in the soft, deep grass the clover
Looked like a button box turned over.

—*Wallace McElroy Kelly*

Dandelions

The tulips and the jonquils
I can only smell and see;
For they belong to Mrs. Jones,
They don't belong to me.

The dancing cherry blossoms
And laughing daffodils
Are just to look at, not to touch,
For they are Mrs. Hill's.

But nature made the dandelions
And scattered hundreds of them
For little children's hands to pick
To twine and wear, to love them.

—*Ann Devlin*

Weather

Outdoors

I love the sun,
  I love the sky,
I love the wind
  That whistles by.

I love the grass,
  I love the flowers,
I love the cool
  Refreshing showers.

I love the snow,
  I love the trees,
I love the summer's
  Cooling breeze.

I love the rain
  That pours and pours.
I love most every-
  Thing outdoors.

—*Vivian G. Gouled*

The Wind

The wind makes friends with my balloons
  And likes to come and play—
They have the very best of times
  Upon a blustery day.

He tries in every way he can
  To get them from my hand—
First blows on that side, then on this—
  They seem to understand.

When finally he sets one free,
  I hear him laugh out loud—
Away he takes it flying fast
  And hides it in a cloud.

—*Lucy A. K. Adee*

Something

Something sounds like ocean waves;
Something shrieks and groans and raves;
Something whistles past at night;
Something tussles with my kite;
Something cries at windowpanes;
Something howls in sudden rains.
Have you guessed what it might be?

Of course, for it's the wind, you see!

—*Dorothy Agard Ansley*

The West Wind's Cold

One day in March, so I've been told,
The West Wind caught a dreadful cold.
First he'd sniffle, then he'd sneeze.
Soon he'd blown up quite a breeze.
He sneezed so hard throughout the day,
He nearly blew the sky away.

—*Claire Saalbach*

An Answer

When branches move
  Upon the trees,
It's just their answer
  To the breeze.

—*Vivian G. Gouled*

Just as they might take apart a toy to see how it works, children can take apart groups of words to discover how language works. Arranging words in alphabetical order, for example, helps them to see that all words in English are some combinations of the twenty-six letters in the alphabet. Have the children list the words in the short poem "An Answer," then arrange them alphabetically by the first letter in each word.

Cloud Caravans

Cloud caravans are passing
In the desert of the sky,
Rounded with packs of cotton,
Like camels moving by.

With steady flow they hump and go
Toward an oasis in the west,
And there the weary caravans
Disband . . . and drift . . . and rest.

—Solveig Paulson Russell

Fog

The fog's a gray blanket
Rushing in from the sea.
It covers each house,
It covers each tree.
Then it blows in the wind
And covers up me!

—Enola Chamberlin

Using the poems on these two pages, continue the alphabetizing lesson beyond the first letter. Have the children list the words in the poem "Fog" and then alphabetize them to the second letter. This exercise shows children how a telephone book is created. You may want to share pages of any directory, including the class list, to demonstrate how alphabetizing is part of everyday life.

Lambs

White lambs are in the sky today.
They skip, they jump, they run.
One is far off by himself,
Lying in the sun.

The wind comes up and rustles past.
The lambs run to their mother.
So close they are, it's hard to tell
One lambkin from another.

The mother starts to leave them now.
I wait; and by and by
She beckons to her little lambs,
Who race across the sky.

—*Alice Cope Wills*

Storm

I like the rather scary fun
Of thunder crashing in the night.
It's like a roller coaster falling—
That chilly feeling of delight.

The curtains blow, the rain comes down.
I shiver, giggling, in my bed
When lightning shows up sky and town
And thunder grumbles overhead.

—*Marion Blyth*

In the Rain

When I come home from school
  Upon a rainy day,
I raise my red umbrella
  And take the longest way.

Umbrellas always dance
  Along the shining street,
Bowing here and bowing there
  To friends they wish to greet.

Puddles are an odd part
  Of every rainy day;
For though I try to skip them,
  They're always in the way.

—*Lucia Cabot*

Raindrops

What's that pitter-patter
  On the windowpane?
What can be the matter?
  Is it drops of rain
Making all that clatter?
  Playing tag again?

—*Mary Spence*

62

Rainproof

When rain is falling
   From the sky,
A raincoat keeps
   Our Johnny dry.
When rain makes puddles
   In the street,
Our boy wears rubbers
   On his feet.
Add an umbrella
   For a roof,
And John's completely
   Waterproof.

—*Marguerite Gode*

Rain

Rain on the grass,
   Rain on the tree,
Rain on the blossoms,
   And rain on—me!

—*Ivy O. Eastwick*

Double letters are another structural form found in English. In the word *umbrella*, ("In the Rain," page 62), the first *l* is pronounced with the second syllable and the second *l* with the third syllable. In *school, street, greet,* and *odd,* only one of the double letters in each word is pronounced. Ask the children to select words with double letters and show when the double letters divide by syllables and when they do not.

Rainy Day

It's raining in the city
  And in the country, too.
There isn't anyplace to go
  Or anything to do.

It's swashing in the garden
  And splashing in the lane.
And all the wishing I can do
  Will never stop the rain.

—*Harriet Evatt*

Puddles

I sort of wish that all year round
Some squishy puddles could be found—
The kind I like to splash and plop
With nobody near to make me stop!

—*Bernice Webster*

Playing with the structure of language draws attention to its elements and increases the enjoyment of words. In "Rainy Day," above, ask the children to locate the contractions (two *it's* and one *isn't*). Then have them read the poem without using contractions. Reversing this procedure with "Puddles," use a contraction wherever possible (*I'd* for *I* in two places).

Rainfall

I like rains that patter
On the roof at night.
The raindrops make a joyful chatter,
Saying everything is right.

I like rains soft and steady,
Those that make the gardens grow.
I like rains that, when I'm ready,
Stop and let the sunbeams show.

—*Esther Freshman*

Three Little Snowflakes

Said the first little snowflake
As he whirled down from the sky,
"I'll light on that red chimney.
It looks very nice and high."

Said the second little snowflake,
"Oh, that is not for me.
I shall feel much safer
In the old apple tree."

Said the third little snowflake,
"Through the air I'll skim
Till I light on some boy's shoulder.
Then I'll go to school with him!"

—*Maude K. Fryer*

First Snowfall

The snow's coming down like feathers;
 The lights of the village gleam.
As I watch through the mist, I see them
 As small as a firefly's beam.

The snow's coming down like feathers
 And soon will be drifted deep.
Tomorrow I'll make me a snowman;
 Tonight I must go to sleep.

—*Harriet Evatt*

A Question

What I would like to learn is this:
 (Does any grown-up person know?)
If there's a rainbow after rain,
 Why not a snowbow after snow?

—*Bernice G. Anderson*

Compound words are common in English. In "Three Little Snowflakes," *snowflake* (*snow* and *flake*) is an example. Have the children find the number of times the word *snowflake* appears in the poem (three). In "A Question," the children should be able to locate and read two different compound words. Keeping a list of other compound words found in reading throughout the day will reinforce how frequently they are used.

Weather

Old Mrs. Rain and old Mrs. Sun
  Lived in a house together.
All day long they sewed and sewed
  On a quilt of patchwork weather.

Old Mrs. Rain stitched blocks of gray,
  Till her stiff old thumbs were weary,
And the patchwork quilt grew drab and dull
  Like a day that is dark and dreary.

Then old Mrs. Sun cried, "Mercy me!
  We must make it a bit more shining!"
So she turned the whole quilt inside out
  And added a silver lining.

And that is why, on a summer's day,
  We may have both kinds of weather.
For old Mrs. Rain and old Mrs. Sun
  Made the patchwork quilt together.

—Edith Hadley Butterfield

Humor

Spelling

You don't spell *penny*
The way you spell *any*.
The ending of *nickel*
Is different from *pickle*.
You cannot spell *bun*
The way you spell *won*.
You wrestle with *busy*
Until you are dizzy.
It makes your head hurt
To try to spell *dirt*.
Let me tell you, honey,
Spelling can be funny.

—*Anonymous*

Lost

Though Mother couldn't find me,
  I wasn't lost because
All the time she looked for me,
  I knew just where I was!

—Frances S. Copley

How Tommy Lost His Tongue

"Tommy lost his tongue today,
And I'm afraid it's lost to stay."
Thus said sister Sue to Mother,
Speaking of her little brother,
When they came from school at noon.
Said Mama, "He'll find it soon."
"Not this time, I guess," said Sue,
"'Cause he lost it from his shoe."

—Dora Marchant Conger

As children mature, they are required to depend more and more on reading silently, and it is wise to begin this practice early. Ask the children to read these poems silently and encourage them to react (within reason) as they are reading—laugh if something is funny, groan if it isn't. When the classroom erupts in giggles, the teacher can feel confident that at least some of the children understand what they are reading.

Shopping

I cannot remember!
  Now what can it be?
Was it sugar or coffee,
  Molasses or tea,
Potatoes or lemons,
  Bananas or spice?
Perhaps it was mustard
  Or flour or rice.
Was it scraps for the cat
  Or for doggy, a bone?
It's surely important
  To shop all alone!
It wasn't a broom
  To sweep up the floor,
For Mother already
  Has three brooms or more.
But it has to be something;
  So I think it best be,
"Please, Mr. Groceryman,
  Cookies for me!"

—*Grace B. Hilton*

My Cousin and I

"To whom are you waving?"
My cousin said to me.

"I'm waving to a mermaid
Who's swimming in the sea."

"To whom are you talking?"
My cousin said to me.

"I'm talking to the white horse
That gallops on the sea."

She did not see the mermaid;
She did not see the horse.

And all because she did not
Believe in them, of course.

—*Ivy O. Eastwick*

Sticky Fingers

"If you linger
near my finger,"
said the baby to the jam,
"you'll get chummy
with my tummy—
that's the kind of girl I am!"

—*Strickland Gillilan*

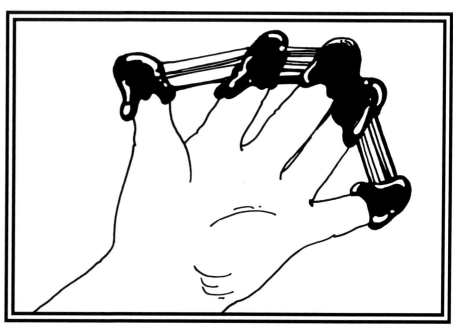

72

My Shoes

Before I jump into my bed,
Before I dim my light,
I put my shoes together
So they can talk at night.

I'm sure they would be lonely
If I tossed one here, one there.
So I put my shoes together,
For they are a friendly pair.

—*Mary Newman*

Nicknames

My mother calls me Teddy.
  My father calls me Ted.
My friends call me Carrots
  Because my hair is red.

—*Anne Jesty Rogers*

Humorous poetry is particularly easy for children to remember. They also enjoy
sharing a funny poem with others as they would a good joke. Ask each child to pick out
a poem from this section to share with family members or a friend. Ask the children
why they chose their poems and why they think their families or friends would like them.

A Puzzle

When I am sound asleep at night,
  I think my clothes start playing tricks,
For in the morning when I wake,
  They're always in an awful fix.

When I place them upon a chair,
  I'm sure that they are right side out,
But when I'm sound asleep, of course,
  I don't know what they are about.

And when I dress, I have to spend
  Ten minutes more than I should do,
Because each thing I must put on
  Somehow or other is wrong side to.

I know my clothes get pretty tired
  From chasing round all day with me,
So why they can't behave at night
  Is something that I cannot see.

—*Myrtle Cox Hinchliff*

While they are reading silently, observe the children to see if any are moving their lips. Initially, most children do this when they attempt to read silently. This habit—and it becomes progressively harder to eliminate—slows a child's reading rate by at least one half. A poem such as "In the Mirror" is especially good to use for silent reading because it is short and contains no difficult words.

In the Bathtub

There's something living down the drain,
But what it is, I can't explain.
As soon as I take out the plug,
It starts to snort and go, "*Ug-glugg.*"
I hear it saying, "*Gup-gup-gup,*"
As it drinks the dirty water up.
It's strange is what I'm thinking,
'Cause bath water's not so good for drinking.

—*Dorothy Landis*

In the Mirror

When I look in my mirror,
What do I see?
A little girl
Who looks like me!

After I turn my
Mirror around,
That little girl
Cannot be found!

Now where do you think
That little girl goes?
I wonder if anyone
Really knows.

—*Mae Taylor Krouse*

75

Giggles

What do you do when the giggles begin?
Do you squirm and try to keep them in
Or slow them down with a silly grin
Or wriggle?

I giggle.

—*Edith Smith*

It's Funny

Our table has four legs, and yet
It never takes a walk.
My shoes have tongues, but I don't hear
Them ever try to talk.

And windows never
Do complain,
Though every window
Has a pane.

—*Eleanor Hammond*

The Onion Mystery

Under the onion's paper skin
Another onion hid within.
I peeled its coat, and then I spied
Still smaller onion coats inside.
These, too, came off. I stopped because
That's really all the onion was.

—*Ingebord Smith*

The Scarecrow

The scarecrow flaps his ragged arms
To scare away the crows.
But just to show they're not afraid,
They perch upon his nose.

—*Bertha Wilcox Smith*

Humorous poetry lends itself easily to discussion with young children, who are usually more than eager to share their opinion of what is funny. Besides tickling their sense of humor, these poems can help children sharpen their critical-thinking skills. "Giggles" allows the teacher to ask, "What might you do when you get the giggles? What did the boy do in the poem?"

Strange Sights

If cows and horses had to crawl
  Quite slowly on their knees
While pigs went gaily sailing
  Upon the summer breeze
And airplanes refused to move
  Except on wintry seas,
We'd say, with great amazement,
  "What strange, weird sights are these!"

—*Lena B. Ellingwood*

The Clever
Little Old Man

A little old man of the sea
Went out in a boat for a sail.
The water came in
Almost up to his chin
And he had nothing with which to bail.

But this little old man of the sea
Just drew out his jackknife so stout,
And a hole with its blade
In the bottom he made,
So that all of the water ran out.

—*Anonymous*

The selections on these pages demonstrate the use of voice in writing. Ask the children whether they know who is talking in each of the poems. "At Camp" and "Sun Dots" are written from the point of view of the speaker, in first person. "Strange Sights" and "The Clever Little Old Man" are written by observers, in the third person. Children can recognize first person by the use of words such as *I* or *me*.

At Camp

When we had water sports at camp,
My mother came to see.
My trunks kept slipping all the time.
The lifeguard called to me,
"You're going to lose your trunks, young man!"
I shouted, "No, I'm not!
My mother sewed name tags
On everything I've got."

—Dorothy Waldo Phillips

Sun Dots

Have you freckles?
    So have I.
The old sun loves us.
    That is why.
So every kiss may
    leave a spot,
He seals his kisses
    with a dot.

—Grace B. Hilton

Mr. Nobody

I know a funny little man,
  As quiet as a mouse,
Who does the mischief that is done
  In everybody's house.
There's no one ever sees his face,
  And yet we all agree
That every plate we break was cracked
  By Mr. Nobody.

'Tis he who always tears our books,
  Who leaves the door ajar,
He pulls the buttons from our shirts
  And scatters pins afar;
That squeaking door will always squeak
  For, heavens, don't you see,
We leave the oiling to be done
  By Mr. Nobody.

He puts damp wood upon the fire,
  So kettles cannot boil;
His are the feet that bring in mud
  And all the carpets soil.
The papers always are mislaid.
  Who had them last but he?
There's no one tosses them about
  But Mr. Nobody.

The fingerprints upon the door
  By none of us are made;
We never leave the blinds unclosed
  To let the curtains fade.
The ink we never spill; the boots
  That lying round you see
Are not our boots; they all belong
  To Mr. Nobody.

—*Anonymous*

Holidays

Columbus Day

Columbus found America
  In fourteen ninety-two;
But every day Americans
  Discover it anew.

They find its strength and loveliness,
  Its heart so big and true;
And if we want to keep it great,
  It's up to me and you.

—*Eleanor Graham*

Pumpkin Face

I'll take my red wagon
Down to the store
And buy a big pumpkin
To set by my door.

I'll cut teeth and eyes
And a great, wide grin
And a hole in the top
Where the candle goes in.

I'm sure he'll be funny.
His smile will be bright
As he greets all my friends
On Halloween night.

—*Harriet Evatt*

Halloween Cat

Halloween cat with long black tail
Sits yowling on the old fence rail.

Halloween cat with two black ears
Now sees a witch (so it appears).

Halloween cat says, "Is there room
For me to ride on your magic broom?"

Halloween witch nods in reply,
"Come, climb aboard, and off we'll fly."

Then witch and cat ride through the air
On Halloween—a happy pair!

—*Ruth Cox*

Judging by Appearances

Old Jack-o'-lantern lay on the ground;
He looked at the Moon-man, yellow and
 round.

Old Jack-o'-lantern gazed and he gazed,
And still as he looked he grew more
 amazed.

Then said Jack-o'-lantern, "How can it
 be?
That fellow up there looks so much like
 me.

"I suppose he must be a brother of
 mine,
And somebody cut him, too, from the
 vine.

"He looks very grand up there in the
 sky;
But I know just how 'twill be, by and by.

"He's proud of his shine, I have no
 doubt,
But just wait until his candle goes out!"

—Anne Emilie Poulsson

The poems in this section allow the teaching of an important language skill: recognizing syllables in words by sight. Each syllable contains only one vowel sound. In "Columbus Day" on page 81, the title word has three syllables. Have the children read a word and count the syllables. Continue in this way. In the second verse, *strength* is worth noting because, though it has many letters, it has only one syllable and cannot be divided.

Thanksgiving with Grandma

November is a happy month,
Though trees are bare and skies are gray.
We like November, for we go
To Grandma's on Thanksgiving Day.

We count our blessings all year round.
But we are extra-thankful when
Thanksgiving comes, because that means
We go to Grandma's house again.

—*Rowena Cheney*

Thanksgiving

What am I thankful for today?
The hours I get to spend in play;
In some lands children work so much
They have no time for games and such

I'm thankful for my home and bed,
The little prayer I've always said,
But mostly thankful for, I guess,
What Mother calls "just happiness."

—*Lucille Streacker*

An important rule for children to keep in mind when identifying syllables is that a consonant between two vowels goes with the second syllable. In "Thanksgiving with Grandma," the first word, *November* (No / vem / ber), is an example of this rule. The exception is when the first vowel is accented and short, as in the word *giving* (giv / ing). Ask the children to find other examples.

The Wise
Little Turkey

There was a little turkey,
And all he did was gobble.
He ate until he hardly
Could wobble, wobble, wobble.

He ate the farmer's barley,
He ate the farmer's corn.
He grew quite roly-poly
Before Thanksgiving morn.

There was a little turkey
Who gobbled, gobbled, gobbled.
He was so roly-poly
He wobbled, wobbled, wobbled.

He grew so plump and beautiful
Before Thanksgiving Day
He thought it would be safer
For him to run away!

—Nona Keen Duffy

Winter Holidays

Hanukkah and Christmas
Bring very special days
That happily remind us
Of loving, giving ways.

Here a tree is trimmed
And stockings hang in line,
While there with light undimmed
Menorah candles shine.

One child made a cradle,
The Blessed Babe to hold.
Another has a dreidel.
But the ancient tales are told

Of people of goodwill,
Of faithfulness and praise.
These things are with us still
In the winter holidays.

—*Jo Morris*

Merry Christmas!

Santa Claus is on his way
To greet us all on Christmas Day.
His Christmas pack has such a load
It's spilling playthings on the road—
Dolls and drums (all sorts of toys)
For wishful little girls and boys.
And still he has enough to share
For Christmas stockings everywhere.
And as he hastens on his way,
His sleigh bells carol out to say,
"A Merry Christmas on this day!"

—*Grace B. Hilton*

A Christmas Gift

There is a gift a child can make,
However small he be—
A gift he cannot hang upon
The bough of a Christmas tree.
It is the gift of kindness, shown
In many a little way,
To make some lonely child be glad
For a friend on Christmas Day.

—*Marion Everett Hayn*

Shoes and Stockings

Said the shoe to the stocking
When they were out walking,
"I'm much more important than you!
No foot could go tramping
And jumping and stamping
Unless it were wearing a shoe!"

The stocking said, "Yes,
You are needed, I guess,
For walking and running about.
But dear Mr. Shoe,
How important are you
Christmas Eve when Santa is out?

"He does not need you,
Indeed, Mr. Shoe;
But he looks for us stockings instead.
And he fills us with toys
For girls and for boys
While you just stay under the bed!"

—*Elizabeth Stuart*

 Always divide compound words first before dividing the component words into syllables. In "Merry Christmas!" there are two compound words for the children to find (*play/things* and *ev/ery/where*). Have the children list other compound words that they find in this book or ones they think up for themselves. Starting the children with words such as *into, around, inside,* and *another* may help them get going.

New Year's Cake

The New Year
Has a birthday cake,
Which Winter helped
The North Wind make.

They made it look like
Quite a treat,
Although it's far
Too big to eat.

I heard them working
Late last night.
They beat some snow
Till it was light,

Then spread their icing
Smooth and slick
Till all the world
Was covered thick.

—*Nona Keen Duffy*

In "The Baby Year," saying that the new year is a baby is called personification. Ask the children why they think the new year is like a baby. In "New Year's Cake," winter and the north wind are personified as bakers. The cake itself, covered with smooth and slick icing made of snow, is an example of figurative language.

I Promise for the New Year

I will not tease, I will not shout.
When Mom says no, I will not pout.
I'll go to bed when I am told.
I won't be shy or overbold.

I'll be careful of things I touch—
Maybe I'm promising too much!

—Gina M. Bell

The Baby Year

In picture books the New Year looks
    Just like a little baby;
So once I stayed up very late
    Because I thought that maybe
I'd see the New Year coming in.

Instead, I heard a dreadful din
Of many horns and whistles blowing
And saw the bright confetti snowing
Upon the ladies on the street;
And all the people stamped their feet
And waved their arms and gave a cheer.
But though I looked just everywhere—
All down the walks and round the square—
I couldn't see the baby year.

—Rowena Bennett

89

To My Valentine

If apples were pears
And peaches were plums
And the rose had a different name—

If tigers were bears
And fingers were thumbs,
I'd love you just the same.

—Anonymous

Valentines

The postman smiles while on his way
Because it is a special day.

His pack is twice its usual size
With envelopes that mean surprise.

There is a valentine for Dad
And one for Mom—think how glad

They'll be to open them and see
A big red heart that comes from me!

—Marguerite Gode

St. Patrick's Day

The twins are all excited—
They want to be on their way;
They're going to a party,
And this is St. Patrick's Day.

They're all dressed up and ready,
Gossoon and little *colleen*
(That's Irish, meaning "boy" and "girl"),
And, of course, they're wearing green!

—*Rowena Cheney*

Easter Joy

Look, everyone, look!
Leaves are lovely on bush and bough,
Robins build in the treetops now,
A song sounds in the brook!

Run, every child, run!
Flowers are shining by hollow and hill—
Buttercup, violet, daffodil,
All bright in the sun!

Bells silverly ring!
With grass and flowers and buds uncurled,
Easter is back in the beautiful world—
Sing, everyone, sing!

—*Nancy Byrd Turner*

Young children enjoy learning about holiday traditions and talking about how their families and their friends' families celebrate. Marking holidays can also help children grasp the idea of the calendar because holidays naturally provide a kind of order to the passing year. With a calendar in front of them, have the children find when the holidays on pages 90, 91, and 92 occur.

Easter Morning

I got a bunny
With very pink eyes
And a nest full of eggs—
It was quite a surprise!

They are purple and red
And yellow and blue.
I think the bunny's an artist,
Don't you?

—Harriet Evatt

Sing a Song of Easter

Sing a song of Easter—
    Lilies in a row,
Baskets full of colored eggs
    Everywhere you go.

Sing a song of Easter—
    Joy for everyone,
Funny little rabbits
    Frisking in the sun.

Sing a song of Easter—
    Robins in the trees,
Daffodils and jonquils
    Nodding in the breeze.

Sing a song of Easter—
    Church bells on the air,
Happy children's voices
    Ringing everywhere.

—Elizabeth Upham

Friends and Family

Twins

They have the same birthday.
  Each looks like the other
'Cause one is a twin
  And so is his brother!

—*Vivian G. Gouled*

Special Friend

Up and down and all around,
There's my shadow on the ground,
Doing everything I do,
Instead of one, he makes me two.

When I run along the beach,
There he is within my reach.
When I build sand castles fine,
There are his, right next to mine.

When I climb high in a tree,
Still he tries to follow me.
But I lose him in the shade.
Can it be that he's afraid?

—May Pynchon

Crisscross Chris

When Crisscross Chris puts on my clothes
   And takes my playthings, too,
My mother looks surprised and asks,
   "Whose little girl are you?"

She hunts for me all through the house—
   Seems worried as can be.
I pop up, smiling; then she hugs—
   Not Crisscross Chris, but me!

—Isabel Chalfant Allam

Good Manners

When Jimmie comes to my house
  (He's the boy I like the best),
I let him choose the games and toys
  Because he is my guest.

Then when I go to Jimmie's
  And he lets me do the same,
I always start with dominoes
  'Cause that's his favorite game.

—*Ethel E. Hickok*

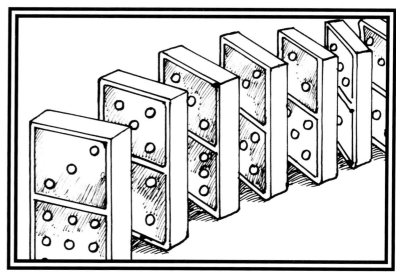

A New Friend

They've taken in the furniture;
I watched them carefully.
I wondered, "Will there be a child
Just right to play with me?"

So I peeked through the garden gate
(I couldn't wait to see).
I found a little boy next door
Peeking back at me.

—*Marjorie A. Anderson*

The poems in this section are good ones for memorizing. "Twins" on page 93 might appeal to very young children because it is only four lines long with a rhyme at the end of the second and fourth lines. "Special Friend" and "Crisscross Chris" have the added appeal of a surprise at the end. "A New Friend" is fun for its simple, easy-to-understand message.

Grandpa's Farm

Grandma and Grandpa live on a farm,
But I live in the city.
Grandpa keeps a horse and cow,
While I just keep a kitty.
But Grandpa says I get to share
In all the farm when I am there.

—*Helen Brosi McLeod*

Common Language

My new friend spoke to me in French,
And I couldn't tell what she said.
When I tried to answer her,
She only shook her head.
Suddenly both of us laughed,
And it was then we found
The wonderful language of laughter
Is known the wide world round!

—*Helen Pettigrew*

Educational psychologists recommend that a child read a poem over and over as a strategy for memorizing it. As the lines become more familiar, the child looks away from the page, looking back only when a prompt is needed. The poems "Grandpa's Farm" and "Common Language" should be read all the way through. "Grandma's Story-Box" and "Fun at Grandma's," however, should be learned one verse at a time.

Fun at Grandma's

Whenever I'm at Grandma's house
    And we're alone, she'll say,
"It's much too nice to stay indoors;
    We'll eat outside today."

Sometimes it's down the garden path
    By Grandpa's flower bed;
Or underneath the apple tree
    Behind the wagon shed.

Sometimes it's in the maple grove
    Beyond the hill. And then
The little squirrels come up for crumbs
    And scamper off again.

—*Elizabeth Upham*

Grandma's Story-Box

I love the buttons in the box
    My grandma lets me see.
She tells the story of each one
    While showing them to me.

The shiny one is from a dress
    The color of her hair.
The tiny one is from a shirt
    Her baby used to wear.

The soldier button Grandpa wore
    The time he crossed the sea.
The red one fastened Mother's coat
    When she was small like me.

I know I never shall forget
    The stories Grandma told.
I hope I have a story-box
    Some day when I am old.

—*Ruth Wilson Kelsey*

Little Brother

My little brother thinks that he
Is very, very big—like me!
He tries to join in all my play
He tries to say the words I say
He tries to catch me when I run
And laughs because he thinks it's fun.

Although he thinks he's big and strong,
I have to help him all day long.
I have to help him through the gate.
He never puts his hat on straight!
So many things he cannot do
Because my brother's only two.

—Mildred Mead

Nothing to Do

If I were Mother,
I'd bake a chocolate cake;
If I were Daddy,
I'd take me to the lake.

If I were Sister,
I'd play house with me;
If I were Brother,
I'd climb that cherry tree.

But Brother's out a-fishing,
And Daddy's gone to town,
And Sister's painting pictures,
And Mother's lying down.

So I am in the hammock,
As sleepy as can be,
With not a thing to do today—
Because I'm only me.

—Audrey McKim

Our New Baby

Our new baby
Has ten toes.
I can count them;
So can Rose;
So can John
(Next door to me).
We all go to
School, you see.

Our new baby—
He's so small
He can't count
His toes at all.

—*Ivy O. Eastwick*

 Relying on meaning can be an aid in remembering. For example, to learn the poem
"Nothing to Do," the child can ask the questions, "What would you do if you were a
mother?" and then, ". . . if you were a father?" and so on. Point out that the third verse
tells what each is doing. Then the last verse is about what the child in the poem is
doing and why. The same approach can be applied in memorizing almost any poem.

Whiskers

Sometimes when he's cut his whiskers off,
My daddy's face is smooth and soft.
But other times I'm in a fix,
For Daddy's kiss is rough—and pricks!
I'm very glad I'm not like him—
I wouldn't want stems growing on MY chin!

—*Jessica Potter Broderick*

Haircut

When Daddy gets his hair cut
    at the corner barber shop,
They don't call him "my little man"
    or give him a lollipop.
Why do they all treat me that way?
    That's what I'd like to know!
There's only one thing I can do—
    that's grow, and grow, and grow.

—*Marie B. Benz*

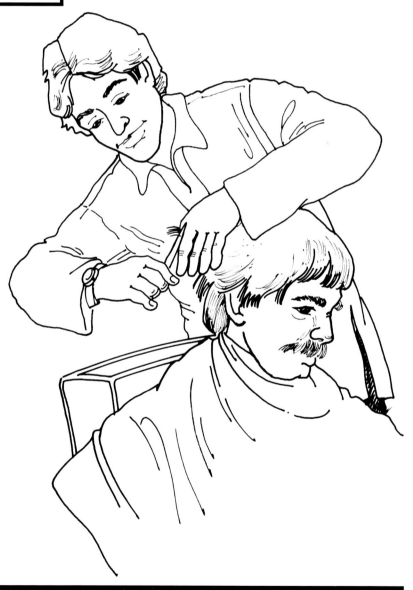

The poems on these two pages are all about fathers. Instead of having the children learn an entire poem, have them learn only one line at a time. In a group, have different children each learn a line (or each row recite a line), then move around the group until each member can recite the entire poem.

Who Comes!

Step, step,
Up the stair.
Thumpity-thump;
Guess who's there!
I hear shoes
And a jangly key.
Daddy's home—
You can't fool me!

—*Marian Burns Darling*

Walking

When Daddy
Walks
With Jean and me,
We have a
Lot of fun
'Cause we can't
Walk as fast
As he,
Unless we
Skip and
Run.
I stretch
And stretch
My legs so far,
I nearly slip
And fall.
But how
Does Daddy
Take such steps?
He doesn't stretch
At all!

—*Grace Ellen Glaubitz*

101

Fishing

Down at the sea
We were fishing, all three—
A sea gull
And Dad
     And me.

I watched the gull dip
And a fish in the tip
Of his bill
Would glisten
     And drip.

And fishing was fine
On Dad's hook and line.
Even I
Caught a crab
     On mine.

Down at the sea
We were fishing, all three—
A sea gull
And Dad
     And me.

—Elsie S. Lindgren

Breaking Trail

My mom and I go walking
In the wood and wade the snow
To see the tiny tracks that point
The way the wild things go.
And Mom says the things we do
Leave tracks that show as plainly, too.

—*Annie Kendall Wilson*

When it is time to memorize a poem, children should have some choice in the matter. They will have an easier time learning a poem if the subject interests them. Children who like fishing, for example, might choose "Fishing." The hikers or snow lovers in the class might prefer "Breaking Trail." Give them lots of poems from which to choose, from this collection or another book.

HELLO
MY NAME IS
Mary Lou
Mother

A Name

When Mother was a little girl
Her name was Anna May.
But we just call her *Mother* now,
Which is the nicest way.

I think that I will change my name
When I am grown up, too,
And have folks call me *Mother* then,
Instead of *Mary Lou*.

—*Alice Stumpmier*

A Walk

I like to walk with Daddy, for
He always seems to know
The very kind of places that
I would like to go.

I like to walk with Mother, too,
But she is very slow.
She has so much to say to folks
Instead of just "Hello!"

—*Anonymous*

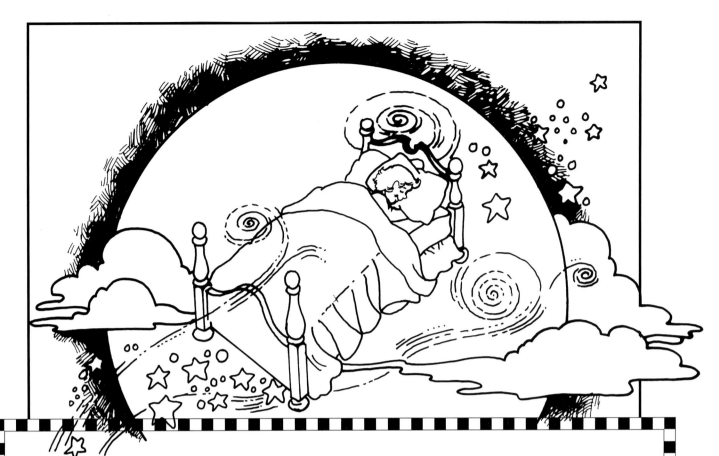

Wishes and Dreams

Bedtime Wish

At night before I go to sleep
I wish that I could always keep
My mind on happy things, not sorrow,
And happy thoughts about the morrow
Until my drowsy thoughts all seem
To slip into a happy dream.

—*Garry Cleveland Myers*

Little Girl's Wish

I wish I were a big, big girl
So I could stay up late.
I do not like to go to bed
When it is only eight.

There are so many games to play
And other things to do.
I hate to have to go to bed!
I'm sure that you would, too.

When I'm a mother with a child
And the clock strikes eight,
I'll smile and say to her, "My dear,
Tonight we'll stay up late!"

—*Marian Kennedy*

The poems in this section can be used to launch a discussion of the children's own wishes and dreams. Ask them which kinds of wishes are likely to come true and which are not. For example, the girl in "Little Girl's Wish" will eventually become a big girl, but the speaker in "Olden Days" is unlikely to return to that time. After reading "In Your Place," ask the children how they would think about putting themselves in another's place.

In Your Place

I wish I often put myself
In your place
With my imagination
So I could see
As you see
And think of you instead of me.

—*Garry Cleveland Myers*

Olden Days

I wish I'd lived in olden days.
  It would have been such fun
To wear a wig and panniered skirt
  Like Martha Washington.

It would have been such fun to set
  A spinning wheel to humming
Or sit down at the harpsichord
  To do a bit of strumming.

I'd play a little tinkly tune
  That no one could forget.
Then everyone would rise and bow
  And dance the minuet.

—*Rowena Bennett*

107

Dream Wings

If I could have wings
Like birds, I would fly
All over our town
Then up to the sky.

I'd follow the clouds
To see where they go,
Find where the rain stays
And maybe the snow.

—*Lenore McLaughlin Link*

The Two of Me

If I could be two me's, I'd like
To climb high in a tree
And look down on my other self
To see how small I'd be.

—*Bertha R. Hudelson*

108

Time for Everything

Dreaming and wishing
Are always fun,
But only by doing
Will things get done.

—*Darlene E. Kardon*

Tree

There is a tree in my backyard
I'd like to climb, but it's too hard.
It's much too high where branches grow
And much too fat to shinny, so
I sit down here and look on top
Where all the little branches stop
And think how fine it's going to be
When I am big and climb that tree.

—*Alice J. Pedigo*

Note that the poems "Dream Wings" and "The Two of Me" both begin with the word *if*.
A good introduction to these poems could be to have the children say or write a sentence
beginning with *if*. Then read these two poems. As another exercise, ask the children to
write a new poem beginning with their *if* sentences.

Perfect Place

I wish I lived where it wasn't so far
From where a lot of animals are.

I have turtles and frogs and snakes and guppies,
Rabbits and mice and a couple of puppies.

I've a squirrel that lives in a nest up a tree—
But that's not enough for a boy like me!

I'd like to feed them whatever they eat,
And take the splinters out of their feet.

On account of the housing, of course, we can't
Take care of a bear or an elephant.

But when I'm a man, I know what I'll do.
I'll build me a house next door to a zoo!

—*Bertha Thierolf*

Poetry is the ideal medium for expressing fantasy. After reading "Pretending," ask the children what they like to pretend. "My Wish" is a reminder that children, like adults, have their share of worries. Ask what they think children worry about, and encourage them to write their own poems expressing their thoughts.

Pretending

Sometimes we like to play that we
Are tigers in a cage.
We pace around and swish our tails
And rip and roar and rage.

Or we pretend that we are just
Some monkeys in a zoo.
We climb whatever we can find—
Most anything will do.

Then we pretend that we are cats
A-hunting for a mouse.
We creep as quiet as can be
And search through all the house.

But when our mother sends us for
Some ice cream at the store,
Then we are very glad that we
Are boys and girls once more.

—*Marian Kennedy*

My Wish

I wish I would never care
When other kids
Tease me and dare
Me to do what I should not;
Or not to do
The things I ought.
I'd like to show
I have a reason
To stick right by
My own decision.

—*Garry Cleveland Myers*

Where Do the Sounds Go?

I wonder where the songs go just
after they're sung?
  And where do the bell chimes
go after they're rung?
  The notes that one hears when
an instrument plays—
  Do all of them scatter in all
different ways?

  Oh, where do the sounds go
when they disappear?
  Is there a hiding place,
somewhere quite near
  Where notes can remain till
they're needed again?
  And how do they know where
they're needed, and when?

  Sometimes, if you stand on
a hillside and yell,
  The notes all come back again,
clear as a bell.
  But where do the rest of the
noises all go?
  If you find out, tell me, for
I'd like to know.

—*Madelen Smith*

Telephone

Elves race through the telephone wires
  To carry the sounds to and fro;
I'm sure that's how the telephones work—
  For an elf has told me so.

—*Violet Shay*

112

Echo

There seems to be a little elf
That lives upon the hill,
Who calls to me from 'way up there
When everything is still.

He says the selfsame things I say.
He shouts them back to me.
He sings when I sing, and he laughs
Like me, quite merrily.

Although I've never seen the sprite,
I found a rocky shelf
And under it a wee small cave—
The size to hold an elf.

—Bertha Wilcox Smith

The Elf

An elf lives
In my garden wall
In a crooked cranny
Bigger than small.
He's a mischievous creature,
Half-high tall.
Sometimes I doubt
He's there at all.

—Lois O'Connor

Three of the poems on these two pages are about sound. Point out to the children that a poem can stand alone or be grouped with others with a similar theme, in this case sound. Ask the children to recall other themes (gardens, family, holidays, etc.) of poems in this book and to suggest subjects they think would make good poems.

113

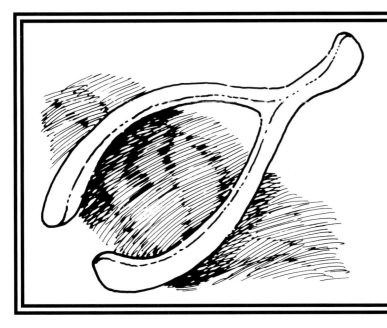

Lasting Wish

The wishes that I wish
Are not of things to sell or buy
But of those things that I
Can make come true myself—
Of things that perish never,
Of things that last forever.

—Garry Cleveland Myers

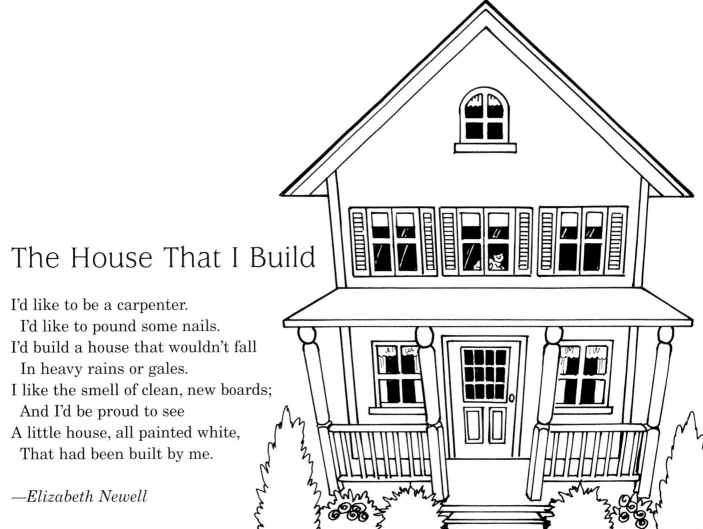

The House That I Build

I'd like to be a carpenter.
  I'd like to pound some nails.
I'd build a house that wouldn't fall
  In heavy rains or gales.
I like the smell of clean, new boards;
  And I'd be proud to see
A little house, all painted white,
  That had been built by me.

—Elizabeth Newell

Poems crystallize the wishes and dreams that occupy the minds of adults and children alike. A good example is "Lasting Wish." After reading the poem, ask the children what they think it means. You might ask them to give examples of some "things that last forever." Talking about poetry in this way helps children understand that a poem can mean different things to different people and yet be enjoyed by all.

In My Sand Pile

A little water I can take,
Mix it with sand and make a cake.
Stones and grass, and leaves and such
Improve the flavor very much.
My cakes are such a special treat,
Good enough for kings to eat.
But if I'm wanting cakes for me,
Into the kitchen I go—'cause, see,
What is on the pantry shelf
I always save to eat myself.

—Dorothy Landis

Baker's Window

A baker's shop is hard to pass.
I like to stand outside the glass
And look at all the bakery things—
Like jelly rolls and coffee rings.

And someday when I'm very rich
(Because I can't decide on which
To take), I'll buy up all the store
And have it sent to my back door.

—Muriel Schulz

115

Daydream

When I am grown up,
  No one will say,
"Child, don't be noisy!"
  All through the day.

I'll be very noisy;
  But folks won't care.
For I'll fight fires
  And help everywhere.

I'll blow a loud siren
  And clatter through town.
I'll rush up a ladder
  And bring folks down.

I'll turn on the water
  Till the fire's through.
I'll make a lot of racket
  And get paid for it, too!

—*Audrey McKim*